Deadly Disasters

W9-ARM-581

World's Worst HURRICANES

Janey Levy

PowerKiDS press.
New York

Published in 2009 by The Rosen Publishing Group, Inc.
29 East 21st Street, New York, NY 10010

First Edition

Editor: Nicole Pristash
Book Design: Greg Tucker
Photo Researcher: Jessica Gerweck

Photo Credits: Cover © NASA-JSC/digital version by Science Faction/Getty Images; pp. 5, 17, 19, 21 © Getty Images; p. 7 Shutterstock.com; p. 9 © AFP/Getty Images; pp. 11, 15 © Associated Press; pp. 12–13 © Christopher Harris/Superstock.

Library of Congress Cataloging-in-Publication Data

Levy, Janey.
  World's worst hurricanes / Janey Levy. — 1st ed.
     p. cm. — (Deadly disasters)
  Includes index.
  ISBN 978-1-4042-4511-2 (lib. bdg.) ISBN 978-1-4042-4535-8 (pbk.)
ISBN 978-1-4042-4553-2 (6-pack)
  1. Hurricanes—Juvenile literature. 2. Typhoons—Juvenile literature. 3. Cyclones—Juvenile literature. I. Title.
  QC944.2.L48 2009
  551.55'2—dc22

                       2008007749

Manufactured in the United States of America

Contents

Hurricanes

Hurricanes are large and powerful storms that happen every year around the world. Their strong winds and heavy rain can cause great **damage**. The terrible power of a hurricane destroys homes, businesses, and crops. Peoples' lives are changed.

The deadliest hurricane in history struck East Pakistan in 1970. It killed up to 500,000 people. There have been many powerful hurricanes throughout history. They have killed hundreds of thousands of people and destroyed whole towns. Here is a look at what a hurricane is and a look at some of the worst hurricanes that have happened around the world.

A hurricane has the power to destroy everything in its path. Hurricane Katrina damaged this church and neighborhood in Mississippi in 2005.

The Life of a Hurricane

Hurricanes form over warm ocean water near the **equator**. First, rain clouds appear. Then, wind spins around the center of the clouds. This spinning storm becomes a hurricane when the wind speed passes 74 miles per hour (119 km/h).

The quiet center of a hurricane is called the eye. The heavy band of clouds around the eye is called the eyewall. This is where the storm's strongest winds and rain are. Hurricanes move from the equator toward the North Pole or South Pole. They may last from three days to two weeks. A hurricane loses power and dies when it moves across land.

The eye of a hurricane is generally 20 to 40 miles (32–64 km) wide. When the eye passes over land, the strong wind from the hurricane dies down, and sometimes there is even blue sky.

Eye

Hurricanes, Typhoons, and Cyclones

Hurricanes happen around the world. They have different names in different places. These storms in the Caribbean Sea and Gulf of Mexico are called hurricanes. In the North Atlantic Ocean and Northeast Pacific Ocean, they are called hurricanes as well. These storms in the Northwest Pacific Ocean are called typhoons. In the Indian Ocean, South Pacific Ocean, and near Australia, they are called **tropical** cyclones.

There are about 85 hurricanes, typhoons, and tropical cyclones every year. Most of the storms happen in the summer or early fall. However, typhoons in the Northwest Pacific Ocean can happen at any time during the year.

This picture was taken during Typhoon Krosa in 2007. Krosa's strong wind made giant waves, like the one shown here, that pounded the coast of Taiwan.

During and After the Storm

Wind and rain from a hurricane cause a lot of damage. Wind blows heavy objects around, and it tears roofs off buildings. Heavy rain can cause floods and **mud slides**. The greatest danger from a hurricane, though, comes from a storm surge. A storm surge happens when wind pushes ocean water far onto the land. People and animals can drown. Roads and buildings can be washed away as well.

Danger remains after the storm, too. Damaged buildings may be unsafe to stay in and flooded roads are unsafe to drive on. There have been many hurricanes in history that have caused damage like this.

A hurricane in Louisiana caused a powerful storm surge that pushed this truck up against a tree.

Pages 12–13: Here high winds are pushing water up onto a road.

The Bhola Cyclone of 1970

The deadliest hurricane ever was the Great East Pakistan Cyclone of 1970. It is also called the Bhola Cyclone. **Scientists** knew the storm was coming, but they had no way to **warn** people.

Today, East Pakistan is called Bangladesh. Bangladesh has always had terrible storms. However, the 1970 storm was the worst. The storm struck at night when people were sleeping. It caused a huge storm surge that flooded one-fourth of the country. Between 300,000 and 500,000 people died. The storm destroyed boats, buildings, and crops. One good thing happened, though. The storm led to better hurricane safety around the world.

The Bhola Cyclone had a wind speed of 140 miles per hour (225 km/h) when it reached land. Here you can see wind-damaged houses in the town of Manpura, East Pakistan.

The Galveston Hurricane of 1900

The worst **natural disaster** in U.S. history was the hurricane that struck Galveston, Texas, in September 1900. No one was prepared for it because there was no warning. The American government **predicted** that the storm would go up the eastern coast. Instead, the hurricane traveled across the Gulf of Mexico toward Galveston. The wind speed was about 140 miles per hour (225 km/h) when it reached land. The ocean rose 20 feet (6 m) in just a few hours.

The hurricane killed between 6,000 and 12,000 people. It destroyed Galveston. The city was rebuilt. However, it was never the same.

Galveston is on an island off the coast of Texas. Because of the low land on which the city sits, the storm surge washed up on shore and destroyed buildings, such as this church.

Hurricane Katrina

Hurricane Katrina hit Florida, Louisiana, Mississippi, and Alabama, in August 2005. It was one of the largest and strongest storms to strike America since the Galveston hurricane. It was also the most costly storm in American history.

Hurricane Katrina caused damage over a huge area. New Orleans, Louisiana, received the worst damage. The rain, wind, and storm surge caused the city's **levees** to break. More than three-fourths of New Orleans became flooded. Hurricane Katrina and the flooding killed almost 2,000 people. It also forced more than 1 **million** people out of their homes. Fixing all the damage will cost about $125 **billion**.

Here a helicopter drops bags of sand to try to stop water from coming through a broken levee in New Orleans. More than 50 of the levees that circled New Orleans broke.

Keeping Safe from Hurricanes

Predicting hurricanes is the first step to keeping people safe. Scientists use weather balloons, airplanes, and other tools to predict hurricanes. If you live in a place where hurricanes happen, your family should plan what to do if a hurricane hits. Make sure you have enough food and water for several days. Watch TV or listen to the radio to know what is happening. Follow orders if you are told to leave your home.

Hurricanes happen every year. Some are stronger and more powerful than others. Many hurricanes throughout history have caused terrible damage. However, taking these steps will help keep you and your family safe.

This meteorologist is tracking a hurricane. Meteorologists study the weather. This man can tell where the hurricane is going so he can warn people who live in the storm's path.

21

Hurricane Facts

The Hooghly River Cyclone struck India in 1737. It killed between 300,000 and 350,000 people.

An 1881 tropical cyclone killed more than 300,000 people in Vietnam.

The Great Hurricane of 1780 was the deadliest hurricane ever in the **Western Hemisphere**. It killed more than 22,000 people on the Caribbean islands.

Hurricane Camille struck the United States in 1969. It was the strongest storm to hit the country in modern times. It destroyed almost everything along the coasts of Louisiana and Mississippi.

Glossary

billion *(BIL-yun)* A thousand millions.

damage *(DA-mij)* Harm to buildings, roads, trees, and belongings.

equator *(ih-KWAY-tur)* The imaginary line around Earth that splits it into two parts, northern and southern.

levees *(LEH-veez)* Raised riverbanks used to stop a river from overflowing.

million *(MIL-yun)* A very large number.

mud slides *(MUD SLYDZ)* Mud flows caused by flooding that travel down hills or mountains.

natural disaster *(NA-chuh-rul dih-ZAS-ter)* An event, such as a storm, that causes suffering or loss.

predicted *(prih-DIKT-ed)* Made a guess based on facts or knowledge.

scientists *(SY-un-tists)* People who study the world.

tropical *(TRAH-puh-kul)* Having to do with the warm parts of Earth near the equator.

warn *(WAHRN)* To tell the public a strong storm is coming.

Index

Web Sites

Due to the changing nature of Internet links, PowerKids Press has developed an online list of Web sites related to the subject of this book. This site is updated regularly. Please use this link to access the list:

www.powerkidslinks.com/disast/hurric/